Neighbors

Jay Nebel

saturnalia books

Distributed by University Press of New England
Hanover and London

Saturnalia Books
105 Woodside Rd.
Ardmore, PA 19003
info@saturnaliabooks.com

ISBN: 978-0-9915454-6-9
Library of Congress Control Number: 2014949483

Book Design by Saturnalia Books
Printing by Westcan Printing Group, Canada

Cover Design: Saturnalia Books

Author Photo: Posy Quarterman

Distributed by:
University Press of New England
1 Court Street
Lebanon, NH 03766
800-421-1561

Thank you to the editors of the following journals where some of these poems first appeared:

American Poetry Review, Best New Poets, Connecticut Review, Connotation Press: An Online Artifact, Cream City Review, Fogged Clarity, Massachusetts Review, Mid-American Review, Narrative, New Orleans Review, Ploughshares, Southern Humanities Review, Tin House, TUBA, Willow Springs, and *ZYZZYVA*.

Some of these poems also appeared in the chapbook LOUD MOUTH published by Steel Bridge Publishing Company, 2012, edited by Mike McGriff and Carl Adamshick.

I have so many friends to thank who helped me along the way to create this book: Matthew and Michael Dickman, Elyse Fenton, Carl Adamshick, Michael McGriff, my poetry mother and father Dorianne Laux and Joseph Millar, Lisa Wells, Matthew Lippman, Major Jackson, Jose Chaves, Allison Dubinsky, Carmiel Banasky, Andrew Frost, Michael Copperman, Heather Ryan, Paul Martone, Keetje Kuipers, Amber Larson, and all of my brothers and sisters past, future, and present at the University of Oregon. Thank you to Jordan Bader, Tom Gayne, Jamie Blumberg Newell, and Posy Quarterman for being there. Thank you to the men and women in the rooms, you know who you are. To all those who get up with me everyday at 4AM: thank you, you are my heroes.

Thank you to Henry Israeli, Rebecca Gidjunis, and Sarah Blake Schoenholtz at Saturnalia Books for your guidance.

Thank you to Gerald Stern for your poems and your big heart. And for noticing.

Thank you to my family for the love and support: the Nebels, Bristols, Keatings, and Hoffmans,
Thank you to my Grandad, Steve Bristol, for his letters. But especially, thank you to my mother,
father, and my brother.

Thank you to my wife, my love, for holding everything together, and enduring. I owe you a headboard.
I love you.

For my ninjas, Maximus and Juno.

Table of Contents

"Talk into my bullet hole. Tell me I'm fine."

—Denis Johnson

ONE

PARADISE

Yesterday a woman walked into a Moscow subway
with explosives taped to her chest
and blew herself and 40 others to pieces.
There was a spark and then,
as if someone had folded the station
in half, they were gone.
Her first name meant *paradise*
though it sounded more like *doesn't it.*
You can find paradise anywhere.
I whisper names when I want a cigarette:
Huntington, Pasteur and *Nijinsky,*
Bruce and *Jane, Paradise.* One of my coworkers enjoyed
branding my arm with a burning metal spoon.
His name was Scott, so plain and American
sounding, so abbreviated, though Scott
read Foucault and rolled his own cigarettes
and played electric bass. In high school
he sold acid to the same football players
who'd beat him up outside McDonald's.
After turning their eyeballs inside out for 13 hours straight
they never touched him again.
We will do crazy things.
Sometimes I would wait inside my apartment lobby
with the lights turned off
so I could scare the manager
out of his skeleton. He and I like Clouseau
and Kato, attacking each other for months
at odd hours of the night. One of my neighbors loved
pissing on his wife, and another worshipped
the smell of manure and licking envelopes

until her tongue bled. I discovered paradise
while smoking pot in a minivan,
until my friend mistook a Buick Skylark
for a police cruiser, shoved my head down onto the lighter
and burned off an eyebrow. At his last public viewing
Abraham Lincoln's eyebrows
had also disintegrated. This is the picture
his enemies would have loved
to keep in the breast pockets of their tuxedos
while floating downriver
on a Sternwheeler. My ideas about paradise
have changed. I feel better knowing
that my friend who seared my eyebrow
weighs over four hundred pounds.
Her paradise sizzles at the all-you-can-eat Mongolian grill.
Paradise in the aisle next to the grapefruit,
next to the cough medicine.
Paradise sucking another man's toes over sheets
of tattoo flash. In the lightsaber and the dinosaur,
in your nephew singing Wayne Newton
through the child monitor, Paradise
entering the station alone,
kneeling down and opening her jacket.

MEN

We're in the middle of it, in the middle
of the backyard barbecuing steak
and chicken. Telling stories

with our wives and girlfriends away,
red and blue psychedelics, Coors Light
and breasts falling into our mouths again

like basalt cliffs into the sea.
Jeremy says, *I did CPR on a gorilla once.*
A girl gorilla, a big one.

I kept thinking, she's going to wake up
and she's going to fucking kill me.
But she just peed all over the floor

before dying on her back
in a room full of humans.
What do you think happens

to the male gorilla back in the cages
somewhere waiting for her?
Do they give him the news?

Slide her body into the cage
so he can smell her dead hand?
Zookeepers, Bill says. *We should grow*

mustaches. And we're gone,
the Apache helicopter of our middle
age flying out over the dunes.

It's not the gorilla that scares me.
It's waking up alone. And I'm not a man
anymore but a paper bag someone's blowing

into to keep from hyperventilating,
the camels long since sunk down
into their kneecaps, the sand everywhere.

THE CLEANLINESS OF PORN STARS

Suppose the desert feeds on a mammoth
sea of algae, a breathing lake
of ferns, the water reaching up at us,
crawling through sand and red rock.
Suppose that in twenty years Phoenix will survive
without the help of neighboring states,
won't need the Colorado or the giant aqueduct
straining its jaws through miles of earth.
Suppose we should drill Alaska
until it's gone. *Screw it,*
my UPS driver suggests, *we won't need oil
in seventy-five years anyway.*
Suppose we aren't headed for the apocalypse
and these desert flowers thrusting purple in my face
are evidence. I've been a fool,
stood on the diving board and refused
to jump, wheeled a shopping cart
through the aisles, my adopted son
dragging me from the list toward strangers
stranded next to the toilet paper
and apple sauce. I want the faith
of the blind hamster who sniffs over the edge
of the kitchen table and pushes off,
to believe as some of my friends believe,
in jumbo neon crosses and radio stations,
in the palm against your forehead,
falling backwards and underwater
revival, in the cleanliness of porn stars,
that when the knife enters the cake
it will exit sans batter and entrails.
I want to believe in the black sand and vermillion

waters in the aftershave ad,
in the smile on the life insurance salesman's face
as he hoists a trophy of brain-flecked antlers
with his clients. I want to believe in his clients.
In an ordinary glass of beer
and the last seventy-five cents in my pocket,
in the black-eyed cigarette girl with an anger problem
who is the most beautiful woman
I've ever seen, in the warmth of my sweatshirt
and the certainty of survival
of the manatees. I want to believe
as my neighbor believes
when he stands out all night in his bathrobe
watering the roses, mascara running
into his mustache, waiting
for his partner to come back.
I want to believe that in an hour
my son will walk through the front door
and look at me like I'm his father.

CLOUDS

We are nothing like them, dragging
the recycling down to the curb every Monday
one slow foot at a time. We cook,
we clean, turn the music up,
argue in the kitchen. But the clouds

cling to the night sky like the dogged
children of nightmares, an endless
rack of evening dresses, samurai
leaning out from their horses
and blotting out the stars.

THE WITNESS

I watched my neighbor pull
himself clear of the wreckage

when his house caught fire. I watched him
like he watched his wife, unable

to move, senseless, the lawn
shimmering underneath the heat.

And would you believe me if I told you
those lungs worked perfectly,

expanding beneath the rise and fall
of his shoulders? The other neighbors

appeared on their porches as if
the sound made them human again.

How his wife's hair must have
looked, fire engraving her scalp

while he stared through the second
story window as if just now

ready to help her. Each word,
each syllable: *I want to disappear*

completely. How it sounds on our lips
as we say it, as if it is some other person,

some other 'I' in front of the mirror
pronouncing the words mindlessly

every morning as we brush our teeth,
absolved of everything.

DISCLAIMER

Consumption may result in sadness,
vomiting, or tremors, in some cases euphoria
when riding in airplanes, the seconds
before impact, whispering 87 Hail Marys
or shouting: *I've never had sex,*
please, I don't want to die.
We do not condone Patient X's actions
or believe his a normal reaction.
Our seamless unbreakable polyester
is meant only for wearing,
do not under any circumstances place in mouth
as doing so may cause a rare disease
originating in rats from Bolivia.
Pregnant women should not ride if susceptible
to spells of narcolepsy, aphasia, repetitive
swearing or sudden obsessions such as wire
cutting, necking, or the spontaneous
desire to cauterize a cousin's throat wound
with a blowtorch. Do not place plastic
over your head or tie rubber bands
around your wrist. The throwing stars
were loosed from the hands of a professional
just as the dwarf and midget
are professionals. The term *midget*
has been chosen by this advertisement
and does not represent the views
of our network. Do not try this at home
with a gas stove or while mowing the lawn.
Always keep your hands
on the wheel. Children must be watched
at all times just as elderly grandparents

must be watched, just as you must be watched
if left in a dark room
with nothing on but a burning life jacket
and a pair of M80s. Call your doctor
if you feel yourself floating
over a field of milk. If you have a history
of affliction you should listen
to our physician and our naturopath
who are both actors
we have paid to speak to you
which makes us not responsible for anything
you may do to yourself.
Black spots at the edge of vision
indicate pauses in the film strip. Seeing clowns
is a common side effect. The following—
Holy Mother of Mayhem, Ghost Limb, Lord of Empty
Cereal Boxes, I have lost so much,
raise me from this hunger for drugs
and women and hallways lifted
in the mist of lighter flame
and smoke, give me strength
when I return to the compass
of a child's face trembling against the stained glass,
lead me through this procession of failed
marriages, bammer weed and downed headlights—
are prayers we cannot guarantee.

QUEEN ANNE'S REVENGE

The oldest child's favorite word is *detonation*.
He turns foam bath letters
into pistols and oranges into cannonballs.
When you're a kid you can aim down the crosshairs
and shoot another human being in the back.
They can writhe around on the jungle floor, convulse
and die, then get up to eat popsicles.
I broke a grown man's cheekbone
and was his best friend the next day.
Two months later we shot bottle rockets
and he burned the sweater right off my back.
When I feel unimportant I imagine taking a bullet
for a friend in a gunfight
and then dying in a beautiful woman's arms,
the whole town calling me a hero,
but that's a whole different kind of violence.
Today, I'm Captain Blackbeard
and I'm renouncing my retirement.
I'm the King of No Mercy,
the Scoundrel of Shark Teeth
storming the deck of an unfamiliar ship,
bow rusted and glistening with barnacles and sea water.
I'm dying with eighteen holes in my chest.
I'm watching, one open eye to the ground,
as my son rips free
from my arms, teeth bared, the breeze lifting
his thin black hair, the ghost mast
wavering above, the Queen Anne gone,
only this ship now, a rusty steering wheel
with snot and apple juice stuck to it,

and packs of four and five-year-old pirates
pouring over us, their gangly arms tangled in the chain rigging,
exploding from the red play structure
with fists full of bark dust.

THE FOOD NETWORK

Plates of roast garlic and prosciutto
shuttle past, the portabella mushrooms
overflowing, pink heads
of prawns teething in the pan.
All this food should make me want
to shove my face through the television
and root around, drunk
on shortcake and apple pie.
I should forget my surroundings,
the running water, the hot iron,
forget the tongue
along the ribs, the little hairs,
should want to dip my pinky
in the Hollandaise sauce.
I should be hungry
but all I can taste is darkness, mouthfuls
of it, darkness in the electrical outlets,
in the veins of the bougainvillea.
Darkness in the nerve endings,
in our organs laid out next to the sponges
and gauze, the scissors and scalpels
lined up on the table like silverware.
Our closest friends prepping
in front of the mirrors, running the razor
over the kneecap one last time,
leaving their houses, the headlights of cars
igniting the slow avenues of space.
The primates of all that darkness
above us, brains frozen or burned
at some unfathomable elevation,

Albert II and Old Reliable, Miss Baker and Goliath,
the pig-tailed macaques of cut off oxygen.
The squirrel monkey whose darkness hurtled
downwards without a working parachute,
the microwave of its body
inside that blackening capsule, its lungs
bumping like balloons
against the ceiling of the ribcage
before dissolving, swallowed into the widening earth.

THE POND

You could come here every night and feed
your problems to the ducks.
The credit card payment and the stolen Trans Am,
the 45-year-old Russian housewife, so beautiful
she's made you into a peeping tom.
I've come to the pond for years
so I recognize the man with the pock-marked cheeks
who dips his head to the water like a giraffe,
the bald yoga instructor jogging in sweat pants
who asked me to fuck him in the ass last week,
and the old woman with the shopping cart
who places a clean dinner plate
next to the garbage can each night
and looks a little lighter under the moon.
They will leave the earth like burning Viking funeral barges!
I want to lie down on this park bench.
My body is heavy. I have carried it here
through thirty-five years of falling
snow. From this balcony tagged with paint markers,
I've witnessed the silent explosions
of countless stars, heard the adagio,
I have been dumb but lucky. I want to rest
next to the other animals making their way
out of the forest to drink. I want to drink with them.
Stare them in the eyes. The rooster
and the wolverine. The bullying geese.

TUNNEL

When my neighbor, the accountant, says
        he could see himself
doing a job like mine, I imagine walking

the long corridor between concourses,
        far below Big Town Hero
and Good Dog Bad Dog, miles of cable

strung along the faceless ceiling like the iris
        ghosts of Christmas lights.
There's little down there but concrete and wire

and a light every five feet or so. A dry, dimly lit
        tunnel dug out beneath the jet fuel
and cargo trucks, beneath blue carpet, seats

and the blue shine of laptops, carry-ons,
        kiosks overflowing with Chapstick
and Kleenex and high fashion magazines.

I'm pushing a hand truck loaded down
        with hundreds of pounds of product,
burrowing through the eye sockets

and bone marrow of Lindbergh and Earhart.
        I'm inside the guts of the thing,
down here where the saints carry

the burdens of their own luggage.
        If there is a heaven,
someone has to work so that others

can drink margaritas as they flick sand
            from their toes and stare out
at the powder blue oceans of Martinique.

A BLESSING FOR THE NEIGHBORHOOD

The ceiling fan in my bedroom warms up
like an old person, complains for a while
before its blades chatter and cough air.
A working fan can make anyone religious
and when I feel religious I say things:

bless my mighty neighborhood,
bless the morning glory, and God bless
the fucking PTA. Bless the conspiracy
of socks and underwear disappearing
from my bedroom, bless the ice cream

truck's music scratching its nails
down the neighborhood's alleys.
Bless the hummingbird's brain
and the colonies of seeds slipping deeper
under the surface of the watermelon.

The Hawaiian shirts inside my closet
beg to be left alone.
The maggots fashion intricate
kingdoms out of the chicken
bones and diapers overflowing

my garbage. Across the street
my Vietnamese neighbor hums Elvis
while picking butter lettuce from her garden.
This world, so much brighter
than the one I left behind,

that freighter of oil and insomnia
overrunning the docks, ripping
through shipyards, dragging men
and women into the air.
I'm writing a letter to the children

in my neighborhood who refuse to sleep,
the little ones in monkey pajamas
who believe in skeletons on the roof
pulling up shingles as they advance
on the upstairs windows. A letter

to my friends climbing the porches
of strangers' houses carrying cleaning solution
and the ghosts of polar bears. My colleagues
and confidantes, my fighter pilots, my organs
wrapped inside where it's warm

and cabinet-dark. To anyone
who will listen, in the kingdom
where I am little more than a mosquito
dropping its landing gear
on the forearm of the beloved.

TWO

MONTAGE WITH PITTSBURGH, JACK GILBERT AND MY KOREAN-BORN SON

So much is born out of ugliness.
My Korean-born son who wore a pink and blue
Hanbok on his first birthday in Flagstaff,
whose birth mother couldn't take care of him,
my wife and I forcing ourselves to make love
while waiting for him to get here,
the bull elk I stumbled upon in a meadow,
half its diseased antler broken off, grazing,
my blind Chihuahua that pulls on the leash
and wants to fight bigger dogs.
The football game I watched last night
between the Steelers and Dolphins.
The way one injured man held his torn shoulder
as he walked off the field,
good arm crossing his chest
like a sling. Fans waving their terrible towels,
overwhelming the stadium with yellow light.
Pittsburgh. The block of steel and ice
rooted in the heart of America.
Once known as the kingdom of potholes
now a romance for high rises and condos.
The home of the poet
who looked exhausted
in his oversized wool sweater, cheap
blue raincoat and thin white beard,
standing before his audience
like a crumbling masterpiece
from the Renaissance. *I just read that poem twice,
didn't I?* he said. *Well I must have wanted
to hear it again.* The stubbornness and insistence.
The recognition and refusal.

CROWS OVER WHEATFIELDS

No anguished brushstrokes, no painter
gone, missing like an earlobe,
no fields with bullets and sunlight
shining beneath the ribs. No fat crows
the shape of M's, no last breaths.
No apologies and no regrets. Alone
for miles, not a person or a house
or the snapped power line of a signature.

Just an abandoned auditorium of wheat,
a few black-eyed starved impostors
flapping their wings over the remains
of my sandwich, and me, the last guest,
a connoisseur of infinite sadness,
sweeping up and down the aisles.

SHOPPING AT MACY'S

Stranded among the white pine and heartbreak
of State Street in February, my wife leaves

to search for a blouse. My chair surrounded
by young bodies, twenty-year-old whips

who will later slip out of the mall in their brand
new cars and vanish into the isthmus, into houses

lit in winter snow. They weigh in, primping
before the mirrors, holding up skirts two sizes

too small, flashing orange and pink hideous
garments, so wild and vulnerable I can't hate myself

for wanting. Under the frill and design of Snap Dragons
the outlines of ribs and shoulder blades startle.

I am nothing to these women,
just a middle-aged married man with tattoos,

estranged in this palace of perfume,
watching them careen toward their reflections.

They are the bright flowers I smell from a distance,
as they disappear into the racks and I am waiting

for snow to fall, enough to cave in this roof and cover
my eyes. I am waiting for someone to arrest me.

THE MATHEMATICIAN

Kurt Gödel refused food and starved himself to death
when his wife was hospitalized for six months,
his algorithms and formulas
swimming around in his brain.
Maybe as his ribs rose like serrated knives
he envisioned the sun locked
over the Black Forest, over Princeton Chapel,
someone abandoning her pickup
in the middle of an intersection, leading a chestnut
mare into a clearing, the sheets
doused with gasoline, madness
galloping through the windows.
He believed someone was trying to poison him
and trusted only his wife to bring food
to his lips. Maybe that's what it means
to really trust a person, jettisoning the rest of the planet.
I hired a woman I believed in
then fired her three weeks later
for coming to work high
on meth. It should have been simple, the merchandise
much too valuable, her jawbone
clicking away at the clock
as I took her keys and showed her the door.
Five hours later we found her
out in the parking lot on her knees,
rooting through her purse, swiveling her head around
and hissing at us like an animal.
Gödel survived Nazi Germany
but he could not escape the empire of love.
My son would let the ocean take me
if it meant his mother would live.

We were wrestling, the three of us, on the bed,
and when my wife jokingly let out a painful whimper,
he climbed on top of me and punched me
with both fists, over and over again in the chest.

ROBERT FRANK: THE AMERICANS

The road bends through the land, worn and frayed
as a pant cuff torn by a dog,
stretches between the luncheonette and backyard,
between the end of the rodeo
and the funeral for New York,
between the public park and the bar.
The cocktail party where hopefulness
is a middle-aged divorced man
boxed up in a black tuxedo
parading women around the room in sequin
dresses, with powdered faces and moles.
And taking them home, lifted on champagne bubbles,
raising their bodies to his in the gray New Jersey light
before smoking a cigarette at the mirror
and asking them to leave. Between the gas station
in Santa Fe where the sun sears the dust on the backs
of the pumps and the elevator in Miami
where a dark haired woman in a milky jacket
raises one eye as she hits the button for the lobby.
The Jehovah's Witness grips a pamphlet, back to the wall,
white knuckled, mercurial. Three drag queens boast
fresh manicures. The shoe shiner, bent over
near the urinals, blackens
a pair of scuffed wing tips.
You know us. We've always been here.
Our elbows tacked to the diner counter, our hair greased back,
cigarettes hanging from the corners of our mouths,
half eaten BLTs and Coke bottles resting
in front of us. We wear Stetsons and lean
against fire hydrants, or we pass by in Cadillacs
and on city buses where we stare forward, hypnotized
by the sound of water slipping from the roof.

We raise combs to our scalps or stand with our hands
in our pockets, attending the dead
wrapped in wool blankets by the roadside
between Winslow and Flagstaff. We've earned rest and work,
this loneliness that flares around us.
At the Chinese cemetery white flowers spread like hair
across the grass and along the parade route
a tuba engulfs a man's face. On the assembly line
a joke is drowned by the bell hammering out the clock,
the whole place flush with dusk. Men in fedoras
hold newspapers over their eyes. From the hotel window
Butte, Montana, fans out charred and burnt.
All around us people mouth,
we've survived, and lose their way
in the mall, forget what they said
just yesterday, the man on Hartford Avenue
who bound a seven-year-old boy
with fishing wire before burying him in the basement,
the schoolteacher who bled herself to death
behind the gymnasium. A woman in a striped skirt
sits in an oak chair in a field overgrown
with blonde-headed weeds,
settling her black hand on her hip.
She is our mother, watching her sons and daughters
pile into convertibles and convention halls, in Belle Isle
and Chattanooga, Detroit and Venice Beach,
the drive-in movie where the wind flaps at a giant figure
pointing a gun in our faces. The trolley crawls
out of the fog, trailing coffee and gin,
aftershave. We're not going anywhere.
Under our fingertips the jukebox glows.

SALVAGE POEM

It was all I had time for.
It had a brain. It had molecules
expanded into the size of fists,

vein-rich magnolias
and war. It had whales.
There was a man near the center of it

who had been shot through
the forehead. He was my brother,
my father. He was no one

I'd ever known. I knelt down
next to him in the supermarket
next to the oranges

and wiped the blood
from his mouth
with my apron.

THE HAPPIEST PLACE ON EARTH IS NORWAY

Portland never cracks the top
one hundred, though many
move here after visiting
between July and September
when the sun is out,
and those same people leave
because the sun is never out
the other nine months, and buy
into the wrong neighborhoods
because someone once wrote,
there are no bad neighborhoods,
and heroin is rampant here,
as are antidepressants, and I use
"rampant" because my mother
always says rampant when talking
about drugs and you know she's
never done drugs because she's using
a word that should only be used
when speaking about murder,
the spread of disease, or Godzilla,
I have friends, Christ, I have friends
who have inhaled pills and syringes,
though most are dead now, my memory
of them opening and closing
like dryers in the Laundromat.

MASTURBATION

Sometimes I feel like a vampire.
        I've never come close
to killing anyone but I have held

my cock in my hands, unleashed
        it like a fire hose
or basilisk, like a little boy's metaphor

for weaponry, and it was private
        and pleasurable as murder
if you prefer that sort of thing.

Tiberius didn't like throwing
        his betrayers off a cliff
but he did it anyway. That's what you get

for ruling Rome from an island.
        Masturbation suits me just fine.
When I was twelve, I pulled off my shorts

underwater and masturbated against
        the jets in my aunt's pink
hot tub. We had turkey sandwiches

and Pepsis shortly after. The blossoms
        this time of year
are magnificent, especially in Dallas,

where Oswald harpooned Kennedy
        into our consciousness
and my left hand unzipped

my pants like a curvy salsa dancer
            beckoning with her dark
nipples and smallish mouth,

throw away your sins with me,
            little emperor, take up
your arms and come to mama.

BLUEBERRY IS THE NATIONAL FRUIT

Shane was wrong. It wasn't the peach.
It was the underappreciated mouse
of all fruit, the purple Cabriolet. The berry
I ate as a two-year-old in diapers
and at nine with my first Santa Cruz skateboard,
and seven days after my mom found
three Sheik condom wrappers in the basement,
the same ones she'd put in my stocking for Christmas
with lottery tickets. When heated and smashed,
we rubbed its blood across our skinny arms and faces
and then rose from the soil like zombies.
Sometimes in high school I'd make out with one girl
to help her get back at another.
Awful selfless of me, which has nothing to do
with how blueberries make a fine addition
to a salad or cobbler, or when cupped
in the hands of a twelve-year-old worker named Juan
in Michigan, he imagines
Nicole Kidman's perfect breasts.
Right now my friend Shane is standing on his convictions
like a sand dune. He's wearing a striped shirt
and sunglasses the size of old women's underwear
and saying something about Duane Allman
and a peach truck. Cut open, the insides
look like brains, gelatinous, white
as the astronaut's space suit
my friends and I imagined floating inside.
Before realizing that someone was chasing us,
someone we couldn't remember, the threat
as real as the nose and mouth of a Hammerhead
knifing out of the black. By then it's probably too late,

which is the worst part, knowing that something
is coming for you, it's hopped up on meth and steroids,
swinging a monkey wrench and bearing down.

MONK'S PRAYER

If it isn't the buildings,
the concrete drone of the construction saw
cutting deep into their bowels,

the birds flying above us,
careless, above clouds of smoke
carrying our souls, if it isn't the streets

lined with cardboard houses
where old men dream
the rain coming down, aluminum

sheets that burn their skin,
or the piano player who cuts
his finger above the wash of jazz

seeping into the kitchen,
if it isn't the snow crushing down
the roof, or the train slogging

on through the city,
its windows dark, passengers
riding blind except for the young boy

flicking his lighter on and off,
if it isn't the man across
the aisle whose throat's been opened

like a can of pears, or the woman
in front of the house fire
who stares back without

a face, then Lord, let me ask
what has conjured this book
of shadows, or this city covered

and uncovered daily,
this dream of ashes I wake to
each day, holding a life

under my knuckles? Let me rest
to the sound of air squeezing
through that man's opened throat,

or the subtle cry of birds, the suicide
hum within their skulls,
O Lord, let me ask again.

SCIENCE FICTION AND FANTASY

A man at the local dive claimed
he'd done more drugs than all the people
who'd ever lived in Mississippi.
I probably ran a close second.
More than the intergalactic samurai
and the centaur, more than any greater-than sign
turned on its feet on the chest of a uniform
and more than any dice-rolling, Reno
son of a bitch. I smoked shake
held together with super glue and drank
a half gallon of vodka while I cooked banana peels
in the oven and smoked their vegetable stench.
Then I stripped down to my boxers on acid
and snuck into the Grant High School pool
and became another creature entirely
after I entered the water, horned and pearly,
throat gilled like multiple stab wounds.
Staring at earth from the deep silence of outer space
must be like this. Forget to breathe
and simple actions become properties
of the surreal. Like sneaking into your parent's bedroom
to steal money one night, being stuck in the closet
as your father disrobes your mother,
enters her from behind and smacks her ass with a belt.
Sounds you've never heard from her mouth,
oohs and *ahhs* your coworker would say
were death chants in the land of Elvendor,
warnings meant to frighten trolls
and large pterodactyls into submission.
Like listening to that Gulf War vet at the bus stop

pointing at cars. Or seeing pictures of yourself, naked
as that sex-hungry astronaut sailing alone through meteors
for twenty-nine days, spill across
the book buyback counter. Or witnessing three men
with baseball bats and brass knuckles
peeling away a chain link fence,
throwing themselves onto your best friend
who has a well known affinity for boyish nymphs dressed
like Peter Pan. Holding him down
and beating him senseless in a back alley
as you glance over your shoulder before deciding to run.

THE IMPORTANCE OF STORY

The general falls, the corners of his mouth
slack, beard crusted with salt and blood,
his hairy legs, which have dragged him for miles,
finally still, his eyes relaxing
into the clouds, fingers caressing the heads
of a giant river of wheat. Most of us know the tale:
a man rides through blackened trees
and falling snow on a pale horse,
his wife and son murdered,
the arena awaiting him. When it is over
we could put on the armor and enter
the ring, we could remember the warm
Spanish tiles and wish for the sounds
of our wife and child snoring in our ears again.
We could lie down and be ready to close our eyes
in the dust. Our stories should be like that.
Stories worth sleeping through the alarm clock,
ones to make movies out of, the double
features worth every hour, every siesta
where we grip each other's hands
and welcome each other to the dark of the bedroom,
our tongues and the backs of our open mouths.
Bach playing one afternoon, Suicidal Tendencies
the next. To the walrus and the widow, to the God
trapped in the chainsaw, to the affairs
and addictions, our curses and loves,
the country-westerns spilling over,
unfolding in our laps like napkins.

THREE

LOUD MOUTH

Caught inside me, an ambulance howl,
a lit match, I've carried this secret

shot into my veins by some junky
in back of a 24 hour diner, built

this kiss-and-tell from the ground up,
kept it alive in the trembling of an Aster,

in a six inch scar below the sternum,
a twelve-year-old boy realizing his cock

for the first time, bedroom door cracked
to the universe, a razor in my hand,

held under my chin, blade pressing down.
I've practiced carefully, so lean in, pull up a chair,

open your wandering eye and your mouth,
take off your gloves. I'm going to tell you everything.

LAWNS

Over blankets and sex,
over money, over the dog and goldfish,
my wife and I are at war.
We're at war and the world's at war,
three of my neighbors angry
at the local church, making signs,
a high school classmate at war
with the Feds, his brain
a brilliant purple mass of PCP.
Every day I'm more like a beached
whale waiting for someone
to pull out his fishing knife and open me up.
We sometimes sleep
in separate beds. We share
the same parking strip, the same lawn.
We watch someone else's child
running wild toward the street.

THE ORDER OF THINGS

Tonight, I smashed a spider
with a nineteenth century Russian
novel for crawling across my desk.
I hate them the way I hated lectures
in college, though I could sleep
through the homosexual tendencies
of monkeys, the industrial revolution
or Kurosawa's *Seven Samurai*.
I hate walking face and teeth
and nose into their webs
where they spin and wrap and suck
the blood from flies. My mother
brushes them into her palms,
escorts them like admirals to the sidewalk.
I know. I'm upsetting the order of things.
I'm drowning the wolf that hunts the deer that ingests the grass
that wants to cover our graves.
My wife says, *Think of something nice.*
I daydream about punching the man next door
for cutting down the hedge.
I wonder if God feels repulsed by the sight of us.
Before bed every night I sweep the sheets
for legions of eight-legged creatures
coming for me while I reach around
hoping to touch my wife's breasts.
One friend pours armies into her garden
from a paper sack to save the tomatoes.
Miraculous! she says. How they multiply, the waves
of spiders growing over the leaves.
My three-year-old came into the study last week

in his Superman underoos, turned off my reading lamp
and said in his tiny voice:
You don't need any more light.
This is what I tell a spider before I kill it.

LION

My friends are getting famous
   and I'm in counseling.

While they're flying around the country
   eating Eagle Snacks and taking on pillows

at 27,000 feet, I'm easing my spirit animal
   into the leather sofa.

Fame, the Impala with the gold Daytons
   coughing and spitting its way through

the neighborhood to your house.
   If the door opens and you hesitate,

you get left behind. I'm not jealous really,
   just lacking a few key synapses

and chromosomes. Yesterday I practiced
   holding my hands like limp dolls

at my sides in front of the mirror
   and saying, *My feelings are hurt.*

The day before, I wrote in crayon
   on the back of a paper bag

while six kids stabbed plastic swords
   into a stuffed lion. Nothing

like a healthy helping of marital surveys
           and happiness exams to lighten the swelling

on the brain. I'm still driving
           my Toyota Corolla into the ground,

still sabotaging the marriage
           with subtle acts of masculine terrorism,

still the one in the surgical mask
           out in the yard whacking weeds while the flowers

get noticed. But the laundry's done.
           It just happens, my friends say.

You're out in the forest alone
           with the bark and moss, working hard with the elk

and beetles, and then someone shows up
           and gives you an ocean liner.

NEEDLES

Thanks, nurses, ahead of time
for shepherding me into the vacuums

of blood. I stayed up all night
to barracuda operas, receptionists

tacking bags of plasma to the pegboard
before calling my name.

Today my veins, tomorrow
the Pacific Ocean. When one nurse

whispers, *Let's try the stomach*—
am I dreaming? That watercolor

of a parasol, the red one, the platelets
those painters are spraying

across the street, my niece's bowl
of spaghetti turning over

on the sofa. Nothing frightens
me more than two nurses

fumbling with my veins
like a pair of jobless teenagers

with a metal detector, scanning
a soccer field at night

for buffalo nickels, cursing
each other in the voodoo dark.

MOTHERS

We were guests in the houses of these Monarchs.
Johnny's mother wore yellow gardening gloves ribboned
with mud and compost, and kissed him on the cheek
before he stuffed a revolver down his pants.
Sid could hear his mother's lips part
when she called from the psych ward
and told him to floss his teeth. His own trips to the asylum
began years later after all night raves, orange Kool-Aid
and angel dust. Every one of us imagined tearing off
Elgin's mother's panties as she stood on the front lawn
in her Office Depot uniform, waving to us
when we pulled into traffic, the sprinklers
rippling under the purple light of the bug zapper.
Her other son ran out of counterfeit money
somewhere in Idaho. Just yesterday a woman with silver hair
touched my arm at the bus stop and told me
she liked my tattoos. She had a mother once
who watched her do awful things. What do you dream of?
The green grass? A piss-stained tiger tearing apart
a piece of rope at the zoo? My mother refused
to look at me when I reappeared in her living room
after seven days. She made dinner, muttering
little phrases while shrugging her shoulders.
The smell of pork chops and onions blooming along her wrists.

KING KONG

The parent company wants to remake
    King Kong but no one knows
what to do with him. He should be

a she, says Angela. Climbing buildings,
    batting down planes to save
her love. No, says Howard.

Kong's still the perfect
    metaphor for the black man.
Taken from his country in chains

and brought here, a slave. Except
    this time White America
gets taught a lesson. You want an ape

to represent Black America? Jill says.
    What if Kong was a baboon?
Someone says. That'd be good,

imagine his enormous pink bulbous
    ass yawning over the city
like a poisonous rain cloud.

What if he wasn't an ape?
    I say. What if he was a child
of fucked up parents? And little Kong

comes downstairs to his father
    cooking up above the living
room table, smoke swirling off the spoon

like a scrawny lizard. What if the boy
          gathers a box of matches,
some lighter fluid and a nail gun,

shoots his father through the eye
          and lights his face on fire, lights
the walls, the couch and dog, goes outside

and stands there in front of the burning
          house like one of those slick-haired
Greek sons from the tragedies?

AMBITION

is more than earning gold stars and more than a bigger slice
on the pie chart. More than toasting
to pink salmon-colored sunsets and sandy-haired blondes
with breasts the size of headlights.
More than backstabbing coworkers with cheap cologne on your wrists
while wearing a silk tie and penny loafers.
More than rising in the company.
More than your father and my father, any father
of a lonely family lineage hacking away at the dawn,
forearms and cheekbones dusted with sweat and coal.
Some men sleepwalk. Others take what they want.
My grandfather would say something like this
in every letter he wrote while descending
slowly toward his death. *You have to decide*
what kind of man you want to be.
One of my NA sponsors had an affair with someone
half his age. He was 28.
He walked out on his marriage
like it meant nothing. When the police came
he was barricaded in a motel overlooking the sea,
the girl still locked in his head, looped on mescaline
and cat tranquilizers. His whole world,
the wife and house, the children and the job, the carousel
swinging around and hitting him in the face.
I watched a man break another's nose over the last tall can
of Hamms. It was Sunday.
We were all broke. It took this much
to wake the rest of us up. When we saw what was at stake
we rolled up our sleeves and joined in.

UNICORN

When Cheryl was six her father went out
for a jar of mayonnaise
and never came home.
The reason could have been anything:
a pack of Lucky Strikes, a woman.
She told everyone in the neighborhood
her father was hunting
unicorns, his voice blood orange
and tentacled, echoing
through the bowels of the shot glasses
she lines up daily like prophets
on the bar. I want to tell her
that fathers have left their families
for far worse reasons.
What do you offer someone
who has lost half of her beginning?
Your father was a tyrant,
a minister of severed hands, a syphilis bringer
castrating the stones of animals.
Wherever he is, I promise you,
the natives are suffering.
Leaving crosses my mind, feigning
mental illness for a younger woman,
that tropical paradise of no responsibility
where mermaids reach up through silky waters
and pull off your boxers
and fire drugs into your veins.
Then a plate shatters in the kitchen
and my wife and son come banging
through the house like one of those furious parades

of dragons during Chinese New Year,
and I put my pants back on.
Once my son is asleep, my wife and I have sex
in the bedroom, not the wild
sex of Olympians thrashing around in the heavens,
but married sex, our shirts and socks
stuck to us like bandages, and, four feet from our window
the next door neighbor strangling
the choke on his lawn mower, kicking the thing,
yelling, *c'mon motherfucker*, when the engine won't start.

FAST, HARD, AND RATED R

I've been working on the right finale,
pulled the rip cord from a blown 747,

an angry brunette at my side
and a case of miniature vodka bottles

under my arm, survived the moon
of 900 werewolf ninjas with a billy club.

I'm the patron saint of driving trucks
into colossal waves of churned earth,

the director of my own disaster,
the soundtrack more frenetic than piano

and strings. I watched a television show
in which a man died while trying to pick up

a newspaper. Now *that* is Mozart for you.
I refuse to be remembered as the mangy

dog that crawled back under the porch
to die, coat pearled with maggots, tiny asteroids

of dried shit and blood. Give me heavy
metal and a long-haired guitar. Give me

John Wayne, four ribs and a lung removed,
pistol cocked and blasting fireworks

over the country like loops of pink intestines.
I want it out in front of everyone,

the aliens touching the foreheads of their black warships
to mine, skulls littered across a field.

THE ROMANTIC

In the legend about the flood, the boy and girl float
under the latticed bridges, miraculously still, their bodies only touching
from elbow to wrist. Somehow they stay together
amidst the wreckage of refrigerators and station wagons,
soggy stuffed animals, wooden houses, eyeless dolls
and picket fences that drift through a city, held together tenderly
as the ash of a cigarette. They survive, get married,
live happily for six months, never fight, make love
on the kitchen tile, until one morning a water-logged greeting card
shows up on their doorstep, a heartfelt *fuck you*
scratched on the inside. He has cancer, only one day
to live, and we feel cheated as they spend the last hours feeding
the ducks on Laurelhurst Pond, because we have to return
to our ordinary lives, snapping your bare ass with a wet towel
on Halloween, or you splitting my lip in a wrestling match.
Or leaving me standing here in a Home Depot parking lot
wondering if you will ever come back with our two Chihuahuas
and new barbecue loaded into the backseat of the car,
pissed because I paid too much attention to the cashier,
my marriage driving away with her hands on the wheel,
music blasting, the wind smashing her in the jaw.

WORLD PEACE

Everyone's dying. More than ever,
dying from plastics in baby bottles, from war
and AIDS and drunk drivers, all of us ingesting
death like hot dogs in one of those eating competitions
championed by a wiry Japanese guy in an AC/DC t-shirt.
During the Miss America pageant
one of the contestants announces she wants world peace,
the audience so silent you can hear
two million groans going off like shotguns
across the continent. More than world peace
I'd send Superman
counterclockwise around the planet like a tether ball,
my grandfathers and grandmothers
raised into kitchen chairs
with aces and hearts in their hands.
Tracy and James and Steve roaring back, the collapsed veins
in their arms and legs climbing like alligators
out of the mud. I'd be in the living room
with Charlie, purple and yellow butterflies exploding
from his rifle, swarming his face and chest.
We would go down to the station
and watch the trains, and when offered,
I would tell him I no longer drink.
He and I and the rest of the world
would do the awkward high five of reincarnation.
We'd lie down in our beds and listen
to our dead cousins breathing like iron lungs,
the ones we didn't like, the loud ones
come back from war and heart attacks and car crashes,
the young woman in the swimsuit and red sash,

raising her lips to a microphone, the rain sliding towards the gutters,
the mice scratching their way into the basement,
my unborn sister glowing in the womb again like a bottle of milk.